Live in Light
or
Die in Darkness

Amariah Ashon

Order this book online at www.trafford.com
or email orders@trafford.com

Most Trafford titles are also available at major online book retailers.

Printed in the United States of America.

Scripture quotations marked NIV are taken from the Holy Bible, New International
Version®. NIV®. Copyright © 1973, 1978, 1984 by International Bible Society.
Used by permission of Zondervan. All rights reserved. [Biblica]

ISBN: 978-1-4907-1886-6 (sc)
ISBN: 978-1-4907-1887-3 (hc)
ISBN: 978-1-4907-1885-9 (e)

Library of Congress Control Number: 2013919889

Trafford rev. 04/22/2014

 www.trafford.com

North America & international
toll-free: 1 888 232 4444 (USA & Canada)
fax: 812 355 4082

Contents

Dedication

To My Lord and Savior Jesus Christ

This day I call heaven and earth as witnesses against you that I have set before you life and death, blessings and curses. Now choose life, so that you and your children may live.

—Deuteronomy 30:19

Introduction
Deliverance from Darkness

Where am I? It sure is dark in here; it's also warm and kind of wet. It is really tight here, and I can barely move. How did I get here? And why am I here? And from where did I come? The more I think about it, I don't even know who I am. So here I sit, in the darkness, alone and not knowing anything.

I must admit I feel helpless and afraid.

Do not be afraid, my son, for I am with you.

Who said that? And where are you?

I am the great I am, and I am everywhere.

Are you the reason I am in this dark place? If so, why?

I am. Because you have been chosen.

Chosen! Chosen to do what? And surely not from this dark place.

> I have created you for three reasons. The first one is to worship me forever. The second is to serve me forever. And the third one, you must seek. The dark place from which you speak is your sister's womb, but you will call her mother, and the place I must send you may seem even darker at times, but this is how it must be.

Darker than this? But how . . . how will I survive?

> Because I am your father and you are my son, and nothing will ever separate you from the love I have for you. No matter where you go or what you do, I will always be there to hold and strengthen you.

But, father, if you love me so much, must I always walk in darkness?

> That, my son, is up to you. I have prepared a place where there is no darkness, where the sun will shine brightly for all of eternity, a place far greater than your mind can comprehend. All you have to do is walk with me from birth until death, and you will share in all the glory and riches I have in store for all those who follow me.

And if I refuse?

> What do you do with a pen that does not write? For a pen was created to write, but if it can no longer do what it was created to do, it is cast away.

 Likewise, when a man turns away from me, he too will be cast away into a place of eternal darkness and pain, a place far worse than your mind can comprehend.

Thank you, father. On this day, you have brought light to this dark place.

On this day, I have called heaven and earth as witnesses against you that I have set before you life and death, blessings and curses. Now choose life so that you and your children may live.

Thank you, my lord, I understand. For me, there is no choice. I have but one path, and that one is the one for which I was created. So from the moment I leave this womb to the moment I die, I will worship and serve only you.

So Let It Be Written.

In the previous passage, which is just a metaphor, Jesus is having a conversation with an unborn child. The child represents all of us. It describes God's plan, purpose, and expectations for our lives.

Jesus tells the child that darkness will not end at birth and that life can sometimes seem even darker.

So what is living in darkness? Darkness is defined as the absence of light or illumination. The Bible teaches us that God is light and that there is no darkness in his presence.

1 John 1:5 (New International Version)

⁵ *This is the message we have heard from him and declare to you: God is light; in him there is no darkness at all.*

So again, what is living in darkness?

Existence without Jesus.

As in all things, Jesus has provided us a way out of the darkness, and it can be as easy as a blink.

Try this, close your eyes . . . the darkness you see can be erased by simply opening them. The darkness of life can be erased by simply accepting him.

Living in light

1 John 1:6-7 (New International Version)

If we claim to have fellowship with him and yet walk in the darkness, we lie and do not live out the truth. ⁷ But if we walk in the light, as he is in the light, we have fellowship with one another, and the blood of Jesus, his Son, purifies us from all sin.

So what is living in light?

A close personal intimate relationship with Jesus.

But what is the path to the light? How do I get there?

First, God has called man to restore his severed relationship with him and second, to have close fellowship with him.

Man's relationship to God was severed when Adam and Eve ate from the forbidden tree.

> **Genesis 2:16-17 (New International Version)**
>
> *[16] And the LORD God commanded the man, "You are free to eat from any tree in the garden; [17] but you must not eat from the tree of the knowledge of good and evil, for when you eat from it you will certainly die."*

God said that sin was punishable by death and that no one who had sinned could enter into heaven.

Because God cannot lie, man's sin debt had to be paid, or none of us could enter into heaven because all men have sinned.

God, because he loved us so much, sent his innocent and sinless son to die in our place.

> **Romans 6:23 (New International Version)**
>
> *[23] For the wages of sin is death, but the gift of God is eternal life in[a] Christ Jesus our Lord.*

> **John 3:16 (New International Version, ©2010)**
>
> *[16] For God so loved the world that he gave his one and only Son, that whoever believes in him shall not perish but have eternal life.*

It is because of Jesus's sacrifice at Calvary that we are able to receive the free gift of salvation and spend eternity with him in heaven.

Because of this, only by accepting and receiving Jesus Christ as our Lord and Savior will we ever be reconciled to God and be able to have a personal relationship with him.

John 14:6 (New International Version)

Jesus answered, "I am the way and the truth and the life. No one comes to the Father except through me.

What choice?

Would a man choose blindness over sight Hunger over food or death over life? Some choices are so overwhelmingly one sided that they cease to be a choice at all.

Living your life for Christ should be no more of a choice than choosing whether to breathe or not; it is what we were intended and created to do.

John 3:3 (New International Version, ©2010)

³ Jesus replied, "Very truly I tell you, no one can see the kingdom of God unless they are born again.

Choose light, choose life, choose Jesus.

First Light

In the introduction, Deliverance from Darkness, God speaks to all of us about his divine purpose for his greatest creation, man. Unfortunately, most of us never accept our true destiny until long after birth. This causes us to live sometimes long and painful lives in darkness. To walk in darkness is to be blind. Blindness causes us to be unwilling or unable to understand or accept something unseen as true. Blindness makes a person to be susceptible and dependent on the whims of others. It limits mobility to the familiarity of that which is known. The remarkable fact is that it takes only a small spark of light to dispel and break up the darkness. If a person stands in a completely black room, lighting a match can guide his or her steps in the desired direction, though not for long, but if one match were struck after another, a path to illumination is possible; the more the illumination, the clearer the path. My life consisted of what seemed to be long corridors, shadowed with darkness. What was most amazing is that I honestly thought I could see clearly, but life had so many twists and turns, and I had no clue as to my direction. In hindsight, how could I have expected anything more from a blind man? The worst part was that my condition seemed to have no end, because as far as I could see, I still saw darkness. I felt I would forever be trapped in the sinister ambush of life. Frankly, even in my darkest hour, I honestly felt as though I had complete control of the road I traveled, after all, I was the driver. I was king of my territory and literally felt impenetrable, and when things went sour, there was always an excuse that landed on the head of someone else failure to perform. God, he had his place, but it was not on the top of my list. I was my own king and refused to bow to another. Sadly, when the misdirected optimism failed, everyone paid, especially the king. I am reminded of the numerous times the Israelites roamed in utter contradiction to the laws of God; they knew to do what was right, but they chose not to. That reminded me of my fight with my spirit man; deep down, I was conscious of what was right, but my flesh was always ultimately at the helm, and whichever way it bent, that was the direction my ship would sail. There is a hovering presence in darkness, a presence that attempts to intensify every wrong decision we make. With every failure, my greatest companion, self-pity, would accompany me when no one else could be found.

One fact about darkness is that the longer it exists, the more disoriented the world around you becomes. Confusion would have sucked the very life itself from me, had it not been for the first strike of light. When I first saw the light it actually frightened me, I became accustomed to the darkness, and it had grown to be comfortable to me. Even though I briefly tasted the Light, it was a doctrine that differed from that which kept me blind. There was a struggle in my soul, a yearning to proceed toward the glimpse of light or stay where it was. My flesh won again, and though I returned to my position of complacency, my curiosity had been aroused, and I could not shake the glimpse of that first light. I realized that my place in the dark world had begun to change. So on I went, but at times, I would stand still and find myself hoping for another strike of light, even a flicker. I rested my hope on the anticipation of that light. I not only hoped but prayed too. Periodically, my mind would rest on the possibilities of a life filled with light, one I never would have thought possible. Interestingly, though I only looked straight into the light once, I beheld the shadow of an unseen life I had never witnessed before. So I continued down the familiar path, believing I would see the light again.

People who I never knew kept approaching me about a new life. It was though they knew I was looking for that light, but I would dismiss the notion; they did not know me, let alone my desire to catch another glimpse even that very moment.

Then it happened, but the light was different this time; the brightness of the light went beyond the optic nerve and senses common to man, and instead, there were rays that penetrated deep into my soul, and instantly, my being was flooded with a knowledge that spoke to everything in and around me. The light had a voice that spoke to the darkness and thunderously commanded it to let there be.

The rays of light spread out like a peacock's display of its beauty. The splendor was almost overwhelming, each beam with its iridescence instantly dispelling the walls fortifying my soul for decades as though they were authored by assignment to my every need.

Every shackle, every pain, everything that seemed to rule and govern my whole life went away instantly.

My corridors were now lit, and I witnessed for the first time a path. For the first time I saw a road to be traveled. I was confident it had an intended destination and, at the end, was my name. With every step, the light would lead and follow me. It was not only clear and plain but also powerful in nature. It had a calming effect on my spirit. The light rendered me strong with every step I took; it spoke hope to a once-dead soul and promises to a broken heart. It helped me find my way and brightened my path, because this light, was *Jesus*. Because of my introduction to him and now through him, for the first time in my life, I could truly see and feel living in light.

Because of my Lord and Savior Jesus Christ, I was blind no more. I could see clearly because my Lord had truly given me my first sight.

Now What?

O kay, so now I understand. I know that my destiny is to accept Christ as my Savior. I know that walking in darkness will be the result of not choosing him. I know that we were all created to worship and serve, and I accept all this as truth. I have asked God to come into my life, dwell in my heart, and guide me for the rest of my days, but now what? What do I do now? What are my responsibilities and duties as a Christian that are outside of the reasons that God had for creating me? Is there anything more expected of me? If so, what? And what should I expect?

Lord, your word teaches us that we are to worship and serve you, but how, Lord? How do I worship and serve you?

These and others are questions that many Christians ask, but unfortunately, they are also the questions that many don't ask. Think about it this way. Whenever you start a new job, the first thing you ask is what your duties are. (*OK, maybe the second*). When you get married, you ask what your spouse expects of you. When you hire someone, the first thing you do is explain his or her responsibilities and/or duties. All these relationships are contracts, and contracts are just agreements between two parties in which each side has a commitment to do certain things for the other. Well, when you accept Jesus as your Savior, you enter into a contract with him, except this contract is called a covenant, but the rules are still the same. Jesus clearly explains the things he will do for us in his word. But what you will notice is that most of the time when Jesus tells us what he will do for us, he also tells us what we have to do to position ourselves to receive his blessings. Here is one example in Malachi.

Malachi 3:10 (New International Version)

¹⁰ Bring the whole tithe into the storehouse that there may be food in my house. "Test me in this," says the LORD Almighty, "and see if I will not throw open the floodgates of heaven and pour out so much blessing that you will not have room enough for it."

Notice Jesus first tells us what is expected of us. Then he tells us how he will bless us. One of the mistakes so many Christians make is we expect Jesus to do all he promised, without having to do anything he has called us to do. Some people have a "You bless me first, and I will obey you later" mentality, which is like going to a grocery store and saying give me the groceries now and I will pay you later. Sounds good, but it just does not work that way. If we are going to live abundantly as God has called us to do (*John 10:10*), it is far more important for us to focus on what is expected of us than to focus on what we should expect. Remember, if God does nothing else for us for the rest of our lives, he has already done more for us than we are capable of repaying or ever deserving. He gave us grace, mercy, and salvation. Though we may try to earn grace and mercy, we can never earn salvation; it is a free gift from a loving father to undeserving children. In the coming chapters, we will discuss what God expects from us as Christians as well as what we should expect.

We will touch on some topics that the Lord has assigned me to share that I pray will bless you on the most wonderful journey you will ever take . . . walking with Christ.

Father, thank you for this opportunity to be used by you. My prayer is that you will guide my mind and hands so that only your words will come forth. I am but a humble servant. Use me, Lord.

Amen.

Perception and Reality

P erception is what we think. Reality is what we know. Perception, for some, has always been a deterrent in making the decision to accept Christ as their savior. For others, perception has made it easier to accept him.

Perception can cause some to believe that true Christianity is unattainable or unrealistic. For others, it can give a false reality that their lives will be free from trials and pain and not have any more troubles.

Usually, perceptions are just hearsay started by people who are not very informed. But sometimes, the Christian community itself creates them unintentionally.

Here is a look at some perceptions and their realities.

Perception

If I accept Christ as my savior, all my problems will be over, and I will not have anymore hard times.

Reality

Accepting Christ does not mean the sun will shine every day; sometimes, things will seem to get worse. What we have to realize is that before we accept Christ as our savior, our souls belonged to Satan. We may not have realized it, or wanted to admit it, but we were dying and on our way to hell. Satan does not attack us as vigorously before we are saved as he will after. So why is this? The reason for this is simple. Satan did not have to work hard to get something he already had. After you accept Christ as your savior, the enemy will step up his attack against you. He wants to break your will and shatter your faith so that you will turn away from God and back to sin. Satan is doomed, and he knows it, and his time is running out. He wants to take as many of us with him as he can, but with Christ on our side, we are already victorious.

John 10:10 (New International Version)

¹⁰The thief comes only to steal and kill and destroy; I have come that they may have life, and have it to the full.

God is faithful and said that he will not only help us in these times, but he will also never allow us to endure more than we can bear.

1 Corinthians 10:13 (New International Version)

¹³No temptation has seized you except what is common to man. And God is faithful; he will not let you be tempted beyond what you can bear. But when you are tempted, he will also provide a way out so that you can stand up under it

God does not always change our circumstances, but believing and trusting in him will change how we respond to them and the effect they have on us.

Perception

Christianity is not for everyone. There are too many do's and don'ts rules and expectations that take away your freedom.

Reality

Man was created to serve Christ, and yes, there are boundaries that God has implemented for our own safety, and we must acknowledge God's expectations for us if we are to survive and be productive. Surviving is to resist negative and sinful temptations of the enemy and the flesh. To be productive is to bear fruit.

Perception

The standards for being a Christian are unrealistic; they expect you to be perfect.

Reality

Romans 3:23 (New International Version)
²³for all have sinned and fall short of the glory of God,

What this scripture tells us is that if sin and failure alone could keep us from the promises of God, none of us would receive them.

Proverbs 24:16-18 (NIV)

¹⁶ for though a righteous man falls seven times, he rises again, but the wicked are brought down by calamity (distress or misfortune)

Fortunately, we serve a merciful God, and this scripture tells us that God knows that it will not always be easy to walk straight in such a crooked world.

(. . . I must pause from my point briefly because I think it is important to focus on this scripture. The content of the scripture goes deeper than Gods acknowledgement that we will sometimes fall but reveals his expectations when we do. This scripture can easily be misinterpreted because some may think it is OK to fall as long as they keep getting up, and this is true, sort of. The problem is that if we only focus on getting up, it will always justify the fall. Then you start to think that you can sin and backslide over and over again as long as you keep asking for forgiveness and repenting, it's OK, which is not true. Sometimes, people can be confused with the definition of "repentance." They believe it is only the acknowledgment of sin, so they will identify the sin, ask for forgiveness, and call it repentance.

The truth is the word "repent" means to turn away from sin, which means to stop. Repentance is like apologizing. Whenever someone apologizes to you, the sincerity of the apology is never determined by what is said but rather by what is done. Although acknowledgment is part of repentance, it is not complete unless there is also change. If you repent with your heart as well as your mouth, what you are really saying is, "God, I acknowledge my actions were sin, God I ask you to forgive me for sinning against you, and God I will not sin against you in that way again." So here are the three steps to getting back up.

Get up.

Repent.

Change

. . . OK, now where was I?)

Perception

A lot of pastors and priests have been found to be corrupt, and the others only want you to come to their church so they can get your money.

Reality

Yes! The harsh reality is that evangelists, priests, and pastors—"our religious mentors"—can fall prey to Satan's worldly entrapments because they are flesh just like the rest of us. When this happens, they must get up, repent, and change. With that said, know that when you accept Christ as your Savior, you do not enter into a covenant relationship with pastors and churches, but you enter into one with Christ. Never let the actions of man stop you from being obedient to Gods word.

> **Hebrews 10:25 (New International Version)**
> *²⁵Let us not give up meeting together, as some are in the habit of doing, but let us encourage one another—and all the more as you see the Day approaching.*

The reason this perception has always been so popular is that most Christians and non-Christians consider the church and its congregation as their example of Christianity. If in some way it is determined that the people of the church are found to be corrupt or phony, then the validity of the church and Christianity itself comes into question.

The rule is to never let man be your example of Christ or Christianity; the only real and reliable example of Christ and Christianity is Christ himself. This point is so important that it will be a consistent theme throughout this book because this mentality is often at the root of many problems we will encounter in our Christian walk.

Read and study your bible, for it is your textbook for life. Let the Holy Spirit be your instructor and teacher. If you obey and trust Jesus, he will lead and guide in all areas of your life. These are only some of the many perceptions of Christianity. The longer you live, the more you will hear. Society is full of religious perceptions; if you listen to them, they can be confusing. The word of God is the truth because he cannot lie, and the Bible is always the place to get reality.

Whom Should I Follow?

How is it that there are so many denominations? Why are there so many different ways to serve the same God? Does God tell us that we should serve him different and separate, or should we be united by the fact that there is one God and one word?

Unfortunately, one of the things that we learn very early in our Christian walk is that because of the differences we have in doctrine and theology (*which are usually caused by denominations or just differences in opinions*), the Christian community is not very united.

As you begin your journey and throughout it, you will encounter many believers who have very different views of how we should worship and serve God. Most of them will tell you that their way is the only one that is correct. Some will even go so far as to say that if you do not follow them, you will not make it to heaven. The problem with this is that it can be very confusing because the Bible tells us "not to forsake the assembly" (Heb. 10:25), so it can cause some of us to jump from church to church, trying to be sure we are in "the only correct one." Here is the reality: there is only one God and one word. Therefore, denominations were not created or endorsed by God. There is not one place in the Bible where God talks about or mentions what denomination we should belong to. With all the different views on Christianity that come from denominations and sometimes within our own church, we have to be careful what we accept as truth. Whenever someone tells you something about the word of God, he or she gives you the word only as *he or she* interprets it. So here is a golden rule. Always *confirm* the word; if *anybody*—your pastor, spouse, mom, friend, the author of this book you are reading, or any group—tells you anything about God, never accept it as truth until you have confirmed it.

1 Thessalonians 5:21 (New Living Translation)

²¹ but test everything that is said. Hold on to what is good.

To confirm something, you have to go to its source. Who is better than the creator to define his creation? Who is better than the writer to interpret his words? The source of God's word is the Bible. Whenever someone tells you about the word of God, ask them, if possible, where it is located in the Bible. Likewise, whenever you share God's word, always try to validate your words with the scripture. This is not meant to belittle those who have been called to minister, preach, or teach the word of God, but to remind us who our real teacher is.

Whenever man creates his own denomination, he assumes the role of creator, and when it comes to things of a spiritual nature that role was not given to us by God. The creators of these faiths have the doubting task of defining and interpreting the word of God, then trying to validate their findings by creating religious laws and rules based on *their* interpretation. When we follow these groups, we sometimes get so lost behind their rules and the group of men that lead them that we can, oftentimes, lose sight of Christ.

15

Who is called among men to be able to truly interpret the word of God? Who is righteous enough? Who has divine knowledge? Romans 3:10-20 says *no one*!

Romans 3:10-20 (New International Version)

[10] As it is written:
"There is no one righteous, not even one;
[11] there is no one who understands, no one who seeks God.
[12] All have turned away, they have together become worthless; there is no one who does good, not even one."[a]
[13] "Their throats are open graves; their tongues practice deceit."[b]
"The poison of vipers is on their lips."[c]
[14] "Their mouths are full of cursing and bitterness."[d]
[15] "Their feet are swift to shed blood;
[16] ruin and misery mark their ways,
[17] and the way of peace they do not know."[e]
[18] "There is no fear of God before their eyes."[f]
[19] Now we know that whatever the law says, it says to those who are under the law, so that every mouth may be silenced and the whole world held accountable to God. [20] Therefore no one will be declared righteous in his sight by observing the law; rather, through the law we become conscious of sin.

The Bible teaches us that no man who is under the law is worthy to accurately define or interpret it, but he or she must obey it. Let me be clear. God does call men to be his disciples, pastors, preachers etc. but they are no more than bullhorns, mouthpieces, and instruments chosen to be used by *God* to relay *God's* message, *God's* laws, and

God's rules, which can only be found in *God's* word and without any affiliation to anyone but *him!*

If God wanted us to be led by a man or a group of men, he would have never taken Jesus, and the disciples would have lived forever. God made it clear in *John 14:25-26* who he was leaving on the earth to lead and teach, and he called him counselor.

John 14:25-26 (New International Version)

²⁵"All this I have spoken while still with you. ²⁶But the Counselor, the Holy Spirit, whom the Father will send in my name, will teach you all things and will remind you of everything I have said to you.

All believers represent the body of Chirst, and the body is one. Your left hand may be doing something that your right is not, but it can never act outside of what the whole body does. Denominations cause the body to separate into many pieces, one part not knowing or respecting the other.

So why are there so many denominations? And where did they come from? To answer this question, we must first differentiate between denominations within the body of Christ and non-Christian religions. Presbyterians and Lutherans are examples of Christian denominations. Islam and Buddhism are entirely separate religions.

Then there are groups like the Mormons and Jehovah's Witnesses who believe in God and claim to be Christians but deny one or more of the essentials that other Christian denominations believe in.

The rise of denominations within the Christian faith can be traced back to the Protestant Reformation, the movement to "reform" the

Roman Catholic Church during the sixteenth century, out of which four major divisions or traditions of Protestantism would emerge: Lutheran, Reformed, Anabaptist, and Anglican. From these four, other denominations grew over the centuries.

The Lutheran denomination was named after Martin Luther and was based on his teachings (*"his teachings" means his interpretation*). The Methodists got their name because their founder, John Wesley, was famous for coming up with "methods" for spiritual growth (*whose methods?*). Presbyterians are named for (*their view*) on church leadership. Baptists got their name because they have always emphasized the importance of baptism. (*Was it the word of God that emphasized it, or was it the Baptist?*) Each denomination has a slightly different doctrine or emphasis from the others, such as the method of baptism, the availability of the Lord's Supper to all or just those whose testimonies can be verified by church leaders, the sovereignty of God versus free will in the matter of salvation, the future of Israel and the church, pre-tribulation versus post-tribulation rapture, the existence of the "sign" gifts in the modern era and so on. The point of these divisions is never Christ as Lord and Savior but rather, honest differences of opinion by godly but flawed people seeking to honor God and retain doctrinal purity according to their consciences and their understanding of his word.

Denominations today are many and varied. The original "mainline" denominations mentioned above have spawned numerous offspring such as Assemblies of God, Christian and Missionary Alliance, Nazarenes, Evangelical Free, independent Bible churches, and many others. Some denominations emphasize slight doctrinal differences, but more often, they simply offer different styles of worship to fit the differing tastes and preferences of Christians. But make no mistake: as believers, we must be of one mind (*one body*) on the essentials of the faith, but beyond that, there is a great deal of latitude in how

Christians should worship in a corporate setting. This latitude is what causes so many different "flavors" of Christianity. A Presbyterian church in Uganda will have a style of worship much different from a Presbyterian church in Colorado, but their doctrinal stand will be, for the most part the same. Diversity is a good thing, but disunity is not. If two churches disagree doctrinally, debate and dialogue over the word may be called for. This type of "iron sharpening iron" is beneficial to all.

Proverbs 27:17 (New International Version)

¹⁷ As iron sharpens iron, so one man sharpens another

However, if they disagree on style and form, it is OK for them to remain in separate churches but not to form a different faith. This separation, though, does not lift the responsibility Christians have to love one another.

1 John 4:11-12 (New International Version)

¹¹Dear friends, since God so loved us, we also ought to love one another. ¹²No one has ever seen God; but if we love one another, God lives in us and his love is made complete in us.

And ultimately, be united as one in Christ.

John 17:21-22 (New International Version)

²¹that all of them may be one, Father, just as you are in me and I am in you. May they also be in us so that the world may believe that you have sent me. ²²I have given them the glory that you gave me, that they may be one as we are one:

There are at least two major problems with denominationalism. First, as I mentioned above, nowhere in the scripture is there a mandate for denominationalism; on the contrary, the mandate is for union and connectivity. Thus, the second problem is that history tells us that denominationalism is the result of, or caused by, conflict and confrontation that leads to division and separation. Jesus told us that a house divided against itself cannot stand. This general principle can, and should be, applied to the church. We find an example of this in the Corinthian church which was struggling with issues of division and separation. There were those who thought that they should follow Paul and those who thought they should follow the teaching of Apollos.

1 Corinthians 1:12 (New International)

¹²*What I mean is this: One of you says, "I follow Paul"; another, "I follow Apollos"; another, "I follow Cephas[a]"; still another, "I follow Christ."* (Cephas Peter)

This alone should tell us what Paul thought of denominations or anything else that separates and divides the body. But let's look further; the Bible says in verse 13—

1 Corinthians 1:13 (NIV)

¹³*Is Christ divided? Was Paul crucified for you? Were you baptized into[a] the name of Paul?*

This makes it clear how Paul feels; he is not the Christ, he is not the one crucified, and his message has never been one that divides the church or would lead someone to worship Paul instead of Christ. Obviously, according to Paul, there is only one church and one body of believers, and *anything* that is different weakens and destroys the church.

1 Corinthians 1:17 (NIV)

[17]For Christ did not send me to baptize, but to preach the gospel—not with words of human wisdom, lest the cross of Christ be emptied of its power

He makes this point stronger in 3:4 by saying—

1 Corinthians 3:4 (King James Version)

[4]For while one saith, I am of Paul; and another, I am of Apollos; are ye not carnal?

For while one saith I am catholic; and another, I am Baptist; and another I am Jehovah's, I am Methodists, I am Lutherans, are ye not carnal?

Here are some of the problems we are faced with today as we look at denominationalism:

Denominations are based on disagreements over the interpretation of the Scripture. An example would be the meaning and purpose of baptism. Is baptism a requirement for salvation, or is it symbolic of the salvation process? There are denominations on both sides of this issue, and they have used the issue to separate and form denominations.

Disagreements over the interpretation of the Scripture are taken personally and become points of contention. This leads to arguments which can do, and have done, much to destroy the witness of the church.

The church should be able to resolve its differences inside the body itself, but once again, history tells us that this doesn't happen. Today, the media uses our differences against us to demonstrate that we are not united in thought or purpose.

Denominations are used by man out of self-interest. There are denominations today that are in a state of self-destruction as they are being led into division by those who are promoting their personal agendas.

The value of unity is found in the ability to pool our gifts and resources to promote the Kingdom to a lost world. This runs contrary to divisions caused by denominationalism.

So what are we to do? Should we ignore denominations? Should we just not go to church and worship at our own house? The answer to both the questions is no. What we should be seeking is a body of believers where the Gospel of Christ is preached, where you as an individual are encouraged to have a personal relationship with the Lord, and where you can be taught the importance of personal ministry and discipleship to spread the Gospel and glorify God. Church is important, and all believers need to belong to a body that fits the above criteria, no matter what the denomination is. I want to be clear that being a member of a church that is a denomination is not the problem but adhering to denominationalism is.

Denominationalism is the inclination of religious groups to practice and justify schisms and separate into different groups over disagreements about doctrinal matters, even very minor ones. Sometimes, it is also defined as sectarianism. Sectarianism is bigotry, discrimination, or hatred arising from attaching importance to perceived differences between subdivisions within a group, such as between different denominations of a religion or fractions of a political movement. Even though the Bible does not mention denominations, it does refer to things that would be their equivalent in those times; the Bible calls them factions, sects, and heresies.

Factions—A group of persons forming a cohesive, usually contentious, minority within a larger group.

Sects—a subdivision of a larger religious group.

Heresies—a religion that conflicts with established dogma.

Since God does not call for these things, they are carnal decisions. Galatians tells us God's position on carnal decisions.

Galatians 5:19-21 (King James Version)

¹⁹Now the works of the flesh are manifest, which are these; Adultery, fornication, uncleanness, lasciviousness, ²⁰Idolatry, witchcraft, hatred, variance, emulations, wrath, strife, seditions, heresies, ²¹Envyings, murders, drunkenness, revellings, and such like: of the which I tell you before, as I have also told you in time past, that they which do such things shall not inherit the kingdom of God

1 Corinthians tells us about division in the church.

1 Corinthians 1:10 (NIV)

¹⁰I appeal to you, brothers, in the name of our Lord Jesus Christ, that all of you agree with one another so that there may be no divisions among you and that you may be perfectly united in mind and thought.

So how will you know if you are denominational? If you have loyalty toward a religious party or group larger than a local church and smaller than the universal body of the saved, you are denominational. Christians need relationships that can only be found in the body of believers. We need the support that only the church can offer, and we need to serve God in the community as well as individually. I have always felt as though your church is one of the decisions you should let God make for you. When we try to select a church, our carnal mind sometimes takes over, and we end up looking for something convenient and things that fit our personal taste, like location or whether the church is big or small. It is better to have a church assigned to you than your selecting one. When God assigns you a church, it may be a Baptist church, but he will not assign it to you just because it is Baptist. Remember, *God* does not acknowledge denominations, *we* do. As believers, there are certain basic doctrines that we must believe, but beyond that, there is latitude on how we can serve and worship; it is this latitude that is the only good reason for denominations. This is diversity and not disunity. The first allows us to be individuals in Christ by not putting him in a box; the latter divides and destroys.

At some point, different people will start asking you to join this church or that group for one reason or another, but you allow *God* to make that decision for you. When you do so, always remember this: Jesus is not coming back for any particular group, he is coming back for millions of individuals, because it is a man's personal relationship with the father that determines his salvation, not his affiliation, or lack thereof, to any particular group.

If we as Christians are not united, how can we unite (*disciple*) the world? A fist is most powerful when *all* fingers come together.

Denominationalism is man-made and should have no place on earth, because it will have no place in heaven.

Follow Jesus.

Purpose, Passion, and Responsibility

H ere are three important words for understanding God purpose in our lives. Each word is very important, but it is equally important not to mistake one for the other. Let's look at each one and see how they relate to us.

Purpose

"God, I understand why you created us. I know it was because you love us, and you wanted us to love you. I also know it was love that caused you to send your only son to die on the cross for our sin. That is why we love, worship, and serve you, but God why me? Why did you create *me*?"

This is a question many people have asked themselves. We have wondered, *With so many people in the world, what is significant about me?*

Everything God creates has a purpose, and that includes you. God made the choice to create you, which means he has a *purpose* for your life.

We all are unique and have been created divinely and individually for a specific reason. Man's creations don't have the ability to choose whether to operate or not in the environment for which they were created, but God's creation (*man*) does.

God gave us the ability to choose. It is one of the most powerful tools we have; as we all know, making the wrong choices can be very harmful. It is our responsibility to decide whether we are actively going to seek God's purpose for our life or wander aimlessly in an environment where we were not created to be (*existence without God*).

God will never force himself upon us. He wants us to seek him for the same reason he created us: love.

The Bible, in Colossians 1:9-10, tells us why God wants us to have the knowledge of his will for our lives:

Colossians 1:9-10 (New International Version)

⁹For this reason, since the day we heard about you, we have not stopped praying for you and asking God to fill you with the knowledge of his will through all spiritual wisdom and understanding. ¹⁰And we pray this in order that you may live a life worthy of the Lord and may please him in every way: bearing fruit in every good work, growing in the knowledge of God.

So how do we find our purpose? Let's look at what I like to call the four P's of purpose: prayer, positioning, patience, and persistence.

Prayer

Everything starts with prayer. The ways of God can sometimes seem confusing. There will be times and situations when we will not be able to figure out what God is doing in our lives and that's why the Bible teaches us not to lean on our own understanding. Sometimes, it will be easier to pray and have faith than to try to figure God out. At other times, he will give us the wisdom and understanding to receive what he has for us. In either case, it will be prayer that will get us through. So how should we pray? Here is what I like to call the prayer for purpose. Though yours might be a little different, mine went something like this.

"Jesus, thank you for coming into my life. Thank you for the grace and mercy you have and will continue to show me for the rest of my life. Lord, I understand I belong to you and that I was created first and foremost to worship you and be your servant. Lord, today I totally and completely surrender my life to you. I submit to your will so that I can position myself to hear from you exactly how I am to serve you. Guide me, Jesus, and show me the way. In your son Jesus's name I pray."

Remember, God is the only one who knows our purpose, so prayer to him is where it starts.

Positioning

This may be one of the most underestimated and least talked about aspect of our Christian walk, but it is definitely one of the most important.

Many of you may have heard or read the following story before, but the message is important enough to repeat.

Upon arriving in heaven, a man was brought before God. God showed him a giant warehouse. The warehouse was full of large crates, and all of them had the man's name on them. He turned to God and asked as to what was in all the crates. God replied, "These are all the gifts and riches I wanted to give you—had you only positioned yourself to receive them."

This metaphor perfectly describes the importance of positioning in our lives. Because God believes in divine order, things in our life must be in its proper place. Fortunately, God has blessed us with a life manual (*the Bible*) that will tell us all we need to know. The Bible tells us in Matthew: 6:33 the first step of positioning.

Matthew 6:33 (New International Version)

³³But seek first his kingdom and his righteousness, and all these things will be given to you as well.

Here God is saying, "I will bless you (*All these will be given to you*) after you have positioned yourself (*seek first his kingdom*). Think of it like this: before our children can receive an allowance, they have to position themselves with good grades, good behavior, chores, and so forth; God works the same way. Before he blesses or appoints us, we have to be in position. If we study our Bible, we will learn that all blessings—our health, finances, marriage, jobs, and so on—will come easier if we are in position to receive them. So how do we get into position? *By obeying the will of God.*

Patience

Patience is a branch on the tree of faith. There are a few things we dislike more than hearing the words "hurry up" and "wait"! But the truth is we have to keep in mind that it's not about our time but about God's time. There will be instances when we will feel as though we are doing all we can to be in position, and things will still seem to be at a standstill. You are excited, motivated, and ready to be used, and it seems as though God has forgotten all about you. At that point, remember the words of the popular song: "When you've done all you can, just stand".

Whenever God does something in our lives, there will always be things he will expect us to do. (*Faith without works is dead*). There will also be things we can't do, and things we have no control over. These things are God's job to be done at the time of *his* choosing. Patience through faith is a very important characteristic for Christians. Sometimes, God will create or allow situations in our lives to develop it. For example, when God tells us to make a move (*do something*), he never tells us the whole plan. We are always on a need to know basis with God. So if you have a plan that you think came from God, and you know how it will start and end, then that's probably *your* plan. God's glory comes from us not knowing how something will end and being in a position to have to trust him, have faith, and patiently wait on his direction.

So how can we attain patience? By trusting God.

Persistence

Know that the enemy will always try to tempt you to give up on God. He will usually try this in times when God seems kind of elusive, so to resist him throughout your life, you will have to be persistent in all areas of your faith.

Passion

Being passionate about God and his work is great. We should be passionate about God, but passion is also a personal emotion.

Sometimes, we can mistake passion for purpose. We can be passionate about our purpose, but just because we are passionate about something we do for Christ does not mean it is our purpose.

If we passionately love someone, we will be passionate about pleasing them. Then our passion does not come from the individual act, but the service itself.

Passion can come from love, so it is only natural we are passionate about God. But we have to be careful not to let our passion for serving the Lord replace the importance of seeking his purpose for our lives.

One of the things most people do when searching for purpose is to look for things in their lives that they like to do, they are good at, they find easy to do, and things that require little effort and are convenient. The truth is that our purpose may be the opposite of all these things. Our purpose is not about us but about glorifying God, and that is not always easy or convenient. So as you seek God's will and purpose in your life, do not let personal feelings and emotions cloud spiritual judgment and divine direction.

Responsibility

Now this one can be confusing because responsibility is mistaken for purpose more than anything. Sometimes, it may be hard to tell the difference between the two.

Most decisions we make in life comes with responsibility. If we buy a car, we have the responsibility of the note. If we get married, we have the responsibility of caring and providing for our family. Society sometimes defines worldly responsibility, but the Bible defines it spiritually.

Matthew 28:19 (New International Version)

¹⁹Therefore go and make disciples of all nations, baptizing them in[a] the name of the Father and of the Son and of the Holy Spirit,

Here Jesus is telling his eleven disciples, who accepted and followed him, to go out and spread his word. When you accept Christ as your Savior, you become a disciple and must also spread the gospel. This makes discipleship a responsibility. Another responsibility of Christians is to worship (*these are probably the two most important responsibilities, but in reading your Bible, you will learn about others*). Worshipping and spreading the gospel are just as much a requirement for Christians as punching a time clock is to the employee. Here is something to note; it is probably not your purpose if everyone else is required to do the same thing. Purpose is usually found in our differences, not in the things we have in common. Your purpose may not be something that no one else is doing, but it will not be something that everyone else is required to do. For instance, we are not all called to *be* a minister (purpose), but all of us should minister (responsibility).

To be called to be a minister means to be a pastor, bishop, or preacher. To minister means to witness, disciple, and share God's word. Also, as you seek your purpose, be careful not to get caught up in something grand. Unfortunately, some people can only see purpose on a large scale. They think if it is not a TV evangelist, mega church pastor, or world minister, it can't be purpose. All these things can be purpose, but purpose is not limited to them, so humble yourself and know that God may have something for you that only he can see.

Remember, purpose is God's specific plan for *your* life; responsibility is the duty of all Christians.

Temporary and Eternal

Mark 8:36 says, *For what shall it profit a man, if he shall gain the whole world, and lose his own soul?*

I was about fourteen years old when I was introduced to Christ for the first time. I remember it as if it was just yesterday. My uncle would have a weekly prayer meeting at his home, and an evangelist would come to share the gospel with us. He asked us if we wanted to accept Christ as our Savior; I wasn't very interested, but my mom made me attend, so I just went through the motions and did what everyone else did. When asked if I wanted to accept Christ, "yes" seemed to be the fastest way to get out of there. Then I was told that God had some words that were evident of his holy spirit, so I babbled something just to move on, and it worked. They told me I had eternal life, then sent me home and everyone left me alone.

For the next twelve or thirteen years, I did everything "but" live for Christ; I noticed that of all the things that were said to me during that time in my life, one word stood out—eternity. No matter what I did, or how much time passed, I could not stop thinking about the word "eternity." For all those years, it seemed like the word had some sort of power that was chasing me, so I just kept running, afraid to even slow down; maybe it was because I knew that if it caught me, my life would be changed forever. Everywhere I went, and no matter what I did, I heard it—Eternity, Eternity—over and over again, until one day it just happened. I stopped running.

I realized later that God did use "eternity" to chase me from darkness and into his glorious light. There I was forced to face the reality of what I was created for, without which I may have not made the most important decision in my life.

When I thought about eternity, the thing that stayed on my mind was its definition: Infinite. Christians have always been comforted by the phrase "and this too shall pass." It has always reassured us that no matter how bad things were in our lives, they were only temporary.

God has equipped all of us with the instinct to survive. It is sometimes amazing what humans can endure when we know it's only for a specified time. It doesn't even matter how long the time is, it could be a fifteen-year prison sentence we can usually deal with it as long as we know that at some point, it "will" end. Temporary can be as short as five minutes, or as long as five years. It depends on how you measure time, but there is nothing temporary about eternity. Eternity means infinite, and infinite means "never ending." To get a clear picture of just how long eternity is, let's compare it to a lifetime. The world average of a lifetime is about sixty-five years. You might say, "Wow, that's a long time!" But when you really think about it, you realize a year is only twelve months, a month is only four weeks, a week is only seven days and so forth. When you compare the average lifetime to eternity, you realize that a lifetime is trillions and trillions times shorter than one second, when compared to eternity. It's like reducing the size of a grain of salt one million times and comparing it to the planet earth.

OK OK, we get it. So why is this so important?

Think about this. What if you were offered a chance to be rich without limits for one year? All that you have ever wanted is yours—money, mansions, fancy cars, yachts and so on. You name it, and it's yours. But the trade-off is, after that year, and for the rest of your life, you will have to live in extreme poverty. Would you do it?

Is that easy? Of course not! No one in his or her right mind would sacrifice a lifetime for a year. Anyone who did would be considered insane. Yet people sacrifice eternity for a lifetime everyday. This is what it means to gain the whole world but lose your soul.

If we see a lifetime for what it really is, which is just a pause, hiccup, or blink in eternity, it makes it easy to see just how extremely temporary everything is in this world. The book of Ecclesiastes clearly shows how we should see the things of this world versus eternal things.

Ecclesiastes is a book of perspective. (*Please read the entire book; it's life changing.*) The narrative of "the Preacher" (KJV), or "the Teacher" (NIV) reveals the depression that inevitably results from seeking happiness in worldly things. This book gives us a chance to see the world through the eyes of a person who, though very wise, is trying to find meaning in temporary worldly things. The Preacher explores mostly every form of worldly pleasure, but none of it gives him a sense of meaning or real happiness.

In the end, the Preacher comes to accept that faith in God is the only way to find personal meaning. He decides to accept the fact that life is brief and ultimately worthless without God. The Preacher advises the reader to focus on an eternal God instead of temporary pleasure.

Temporary (*in this context*) can easily be described as anything that is not eternal. If whatever you are doing, whoever you're with, and whatever you have will not be in eternity, it's temporary.

The problem with the mentality of worldly things being temporary is that most people want to choose which things in their lives they consider temporary. Most people will readily acknowledge things like money, cars, and jobs to be just temporary worldly possessions that should never be placed before God.

But here is where it gets hard for most people. When God said in his word not to have any other gods before him (*which is what can happen when we sometimes put the temporary things of this world before an eternal God*), the statement included all these things, but it was not limited to them. He also included those that are dear to us—like our family. It is easy to understand why this type of thinking would be a problem because most of us don't consider our families as temporary. The reason many cannot accept this concept is because the vast majority of Christians, though they love God and are saved, do not have an "Eternal" mentality.

Eternal separation from God is hell, and none of us will know the full potential of living until we get to heaven. Unbelievers believe that the worldly unconscious state of death is the end. Christians know that physical death is only the end of life on earth. But when does eternity start? Most will agree that it is after physical death. This is true if only looked at from a strictly physical perspective. If we go deeper, we will see how it should actually start in our minds after we accept Christ as our savior. Even though our renewed body that the Bible talks about in revelations will not dwell in eternity until we die, or until Jesus returns, we should have an "Eternal mentality" as soon as we accept Christ as our Savior. To have an Eternal mentality, you must have a renewed mind. The word renewed means to restore to a new condition or to be made new. It simply means to change our mind and heart so that we view all things in this world from the spiritual perspective of God, rather than the worldly perspective of man.

If having an Eternal mentality means to see things the way God sees them, then not having one means seeing things through the eyes of the world, which may cause us to react to things the way the world does. The Bible teaches us not to be conformed by the ways and thinking of the world.

Romans 12:2 (New King James Version)

² *And do not be conformed to this world, but be transformed by the renewing of your mind, that you may prove what is that good and acceptable and perfect will of God*

When we think about time with a "worldly mentality," we will always compare it to a lifetime, and everything seems like a long time. With an Eternal mentality, we will always compare time to eternity, and years start to seem like seconds.

When you see time the way God does, you realize two very important points. (1) You have never suffered for as long as you thought, and (2) you do not have as much time as you think.

An Eternal mentality allows us to see all things differently, including our families. When we look at our spouses and children, we will see our siblings because spouses and children are temporary, and siblings are eternal.

The point here is to drive home the importance of understanding the difference between seeing things from the perspective of God and not of man. If we see things the way God sees them, it will affect the choices we make and how we respond to the things of this world. Here is an example of the insight an Eternal mentality can give us. Let's look at the difference between pleasure and happiness. One is temporary and the other is eternal.

There is a difference between pleasure and happiness. Without an Eternal mentality, many of us will spend our whole lives trying to find happiness in things that were only meant to give us pleasure. We believe that if we get a college degree, a great paying job, a house on the hill, and marry the man or woman of our dreams, we will be happy forever.

Because we think these things are tied to our happiness and don't realize they are temporary gifts that were only meant to give us pleasure, they become the most important things in our lives. We become so obsessed with them that we will fight for our marriages, endure on our jobs, and cherish our homes and worldly possessions so much until Jesus becomes only an afterthought. But life sometimes has a way of bringing us back to reality. First, our spouse gives us a letter of divorce, our jobs lay us off, and the banks foreclose on our homes. It's then we realize how meaningless and temporary all the pleasures in this world are.

Happiness is eternal because it is a state of mind based on who and what we are, not on what you have or what you have accomplished. Our accomplishments and possessions may give us pleasure, but *true* happiness can only come from a *relationship with the father.* This example further illustrates the point of Ecclesiastes.

Knowing the difference between things that are eternal and those that are temporary will change your life by changing the way you see and react to life.

God is eternal and forever; everything and everyone else is temporary.

Developing a Submissive Spirit

For some reason, many people have always struggled with the dreaded S word—submission. Maybe it is the context in which the word is used or maybe it's how we interpret its definition that causes the problem. Whatever it is, it's important that we overcome our problem with the word because to develop a relationship with the father, you have to be submissive to his will. I cannot stress this point enough; complete submissiveness to the will of the father is essential to our walk with Christ. Let's look deeply at the word and what it really means, and see if we can identify why it is such a struggle.

According to *Holman Bible Dictionary*, "submissive" means voluntary placement of oneself under the authority and leadership of another. (Other dictionaries give similar definitions; although oftentimes, the wording will be different, the meanings are usually consistent with the one we are using here.)

When we study the word's definition, phrases like "to take orders from" and "being under the authority" are the first things that we will notice. Phrases like this may be what some of us struggle with.

Society has interpreted these things to be something that is degrading or insulting. But if we study the Bible and learn how God defines it, we know that it has to be our perception or interpretation that *causes us to* accept anything negative about a word God intended to be positive.

So where does the negative mentality come from? Well, let's see. Things like pride, ego, selfishness, and stubbornness are what first came to my mind, and there are others, but the rest will probably fall into one of these categories.

Let's look closer at probably the two most popular and common ones: pride and selfishness.

Pride

Though pride is a common reason we struggle to submit, it is also something we never want to admit. The Bible gives us plenty of information on pride, its effect on us, and why we should be careful not to have too much of it. Here are just a few scriptures you can look up later (Ps. 50:12, Prov. 8:13, 1 Pet. 5:5), but for now, let's focus on a brief scripture found in Proverbs.

Proverbs 11:2 (NIV)
When pride comes, then comes disgrace, but with humility comes wisdom.

Here, God is just generalizing the effect the wrong kind of pride can have on our lives. The reason I say wrong kind of pride is because not all pride is bad. To have or take pride in something we do is good, but the wrong kind of pride can be hazardous to our relationship with God. For example, if you have the attitude that to submit to someone is beneath you or that submission is a sign of weakness (*like I used to think*) or that you are independent and make your own choices, then you will have problems submitting to anyone, including Christ. Remember, God is master, and we are servants; a servant must submit to the will of his master.

Selfishness

This one may be the most common, and like pride, the Bible has plenty to say on this issue. The following scripture tells us how the wrong mentality can sometimes be the cause of selfishness.

> **Romans 8:5-8 (New International Version)**
> ⁵*Those who live according to the sinful nature have their minds set on what that nature desires; but those who live in accordance with the Spirit have their minds set on what the Spirit desires. ⁶The mind of sinful man is death, but the mind controlled by the Spirit is life and peace; ⁷the sinful mind is hostile to God. It does not submit to God's law, nor can it do so. ⁸Those controlled by the sinful nature cannot please God.*

Unfortunately, many of us have an "it's all about me" attitude that can make submission almost impossible. Jesus's life was about giving to others. Everything he did was in service to God for us. To live a life of service is to put the needs of others before yours; furthermore, selfishness breaks the unwritten first rule of Christianity, which is, "It's not about you."

Another reason some struggle with submission is the perception that submission should be based on understanding and agreeing. The thinking is, if I understand and agree with the submission, I will do it. If I don't, I won't. This situation usually comes up in our marriages or on our jobs, and this type of thinking probably comes from selfishness. The reality is that submission is not about agreeing or understanding. It's about obedience and trust. There will be times in our life when we will be asked to submit to things we just don't want to do; it is in these times that we will have to rely on our faith, be obedient, and trust God.

Here is another common mistake we need to be careful not to make; I call it "justifying sin." Sometimes, Christians, especially new believers, have the tendency of looking for the model of Christianity in man. It could be your pastor, parents, spouses, or just someone who is respected in the Christian community. The problem this could cause is that we will sometimes intentionally or unintentionally use these people's lives as a barometer of how submissive or obedient we should be in ours. The risk is that when we look for God in man and see someone who is professing Christianity but not visibly living a life of submission to God's word, we have a tendency to minimize his or her failures to justify ours. Once again, remember, the only perfect example of Christianity is Christ.

There are a several things that are extremely important as they pertain to living a Christian life. A few of them are love, trust, faith, and obedience; submission is also a form of obedience.

The fact that submission is discussed so many times in the Bible tells us how important it is to God. God has called the man to submit to him, the woman to submit to the man, and every man, woman, and child to submit to God's divine will.

Who are we really submitting to?

Most of us will say we don't have any problem submitting to God, but just don't want to submit to man. We think we should not have to be under the authority of another human. Unfortunately, this is a very common perception. But is it reality? Do we ever really submit to man?

If you asked your dad to loan you fifty dollars, and he said he did not have it, then your sister gave him the money to give to you, who then would you thank?

Everything God calls us to do is for his glory and his alone. So we should never personalize submission with its subject or object. Always concentrate on God. An example of this would be our marriage vows.

When we get married, our vows are "about" our spouse, but they are "to" God. So to whom are you really committing to?

Romans 13:1 (New International Version)

¹ Everyone must submit himself to the governing authorities, for there is no authority except that which God has established. The authorities that exist have been established by God.

So again, whenever we submit, it is to the *will of God*, it does not matter who or what the subject of the submission is because ultimately, the submission itself is always to God.

Some people also like to choose when and to what they will submit to. That means they will submit to some things they don't want to, but only the ones they select. This is partial submission.

The problem with partial submission is that when it pertains to your walk with Christ, partial is never enough. Think about it. Can you partially love someone, partially trust someone, or be partially obedient? It just does not work that way; it's either you do, or you don't.

In the eyes of God, partial submission is the same as no submission; Jesus teaches this principle when he talks about being lukewarm in the book of Revelations.

Revelations 3:15, 16 (NIV)

¹⁵I know your deeds, that you are neither cold nor hot: I wish you were either one or the other ¹⁶So because you are lukewarm, neither hot nor cold, I will spit you out of my mouth.

Jesus is saying he wants us to be either in or out. And to him, either one is better than something in the middle, and that's what lukewarm and partial is: "something in the middle." Jesus wants, demands, and deserves total and complete submission to his word.

People sometimes believe that the acceptance of Christ itself is an act of submission. They say to themselves that accepting Christ "is" submission. But the reality is that accepting Christ is a choice, not an act of submission, Jesus never commanded us to accept him as lord and savior, he presented himself and gave us a choice. Accepting Christ as your Savior makes you a Christian, but there is a difference between total and complete submission to God and Christianity. Jesus said that whoever accepts him by confessing with their mouth and believing in their heart will be saved. But acceptance, like obedience, is a separate choice. It is important that we understand there is no umbrella of submission and obedience that is created by acceptance.

Let's look closer at the difference between total and complete submission to God and what could be called basic Christianity. (*OK,*

I made up the phrase basic Christianity because it fits the metaphor Mr. or Ms. politically correct.) Basic Christianity is like getting a C in school. You have identified what is expected of you but have not done anything more than what was absolutely required. Total and complete submission is like getting an A. You had shown passion about your work and consistently went above and beyond the call of your duty and graduated with honors. Both will pass you to the next grade, but one will be significantly more deserving and rewarding.

So how can we be totally and completely submitted to God? By putting Jesus first and foremost in our lives, not just vocally, but in action and deed. The confession of love is no good without the expression.

Read your word and pray daily to find how you can please, serve, and bring glory to his name.

To do this, you will need to first die to yourself, which means to always put his will before yours—not fanatically forsaking your responsibilities as a father, mother, spouse, and so forth, but being sure they are all positioned *behind* the will of God.

In the movie *The Ten Commandments*, starring Charlton Hasten, there is a very profound scene in which Moses's wife has a conversation with his ex. In the scene, the wife says to the ex, "You lost him (*Moses*) when he went to look for his God, I lost him when he found him."

Whenever we totally and completely submit to the will of God, everything and everybody loses a very significant part of us, because that part now belongs to God.

Single: Just You and God

I remember the one time in my life that I truly felt single. It was a day I will never forget because it was the day that my life changed. I was dealing with the resent passing of my mother who was my rock. I loved her so much that I loved her too much. God said in his word that we are not to have any other gods before him. There was a time in my life when my mother was dearest to my heart; nobody was more important, not even Jesus. I always felt as long as she was alive, everything would be all right. There was a calming and healing effect in just the sound of her voice. That is the kind of power only Jesus should have. But Jesus, in his compassion, did not punish or condemn me for the way I felt; he just loved me in spite of it. Jesus was so loving and merciful even though he knew how I felt; before he called her home, he just whispered in my ear and said, "I never promised you she would be with you forever." On this particular day, the reality of her being gone had begun to set in. My wife had just informed me that she was leaving. I felt as though all the walls around me were closing in. I had never felt so single.

Then I encountered the most amazing thing. When everything in my life froze, when I could hear nothing, and when everyone had gone, I knelt down before all I had left, just to ask, "Now what?"

My emotions were uncontrollable. Though I knew Jesus was there, I wanted something tangible, something that I could hold and that which could hold me. I wanted my rock, but for the first time in my life, she was gone.

At that moment, I felt pressure on my left shoulder, and the room seemed warmer on my right.

Because the Bible teaches us that Jesus will meet us where we are, I knew my father had knelt down beside me and placed his arms around me. From that moment and for the rest of my life, I knew that no matter what happened or whatever I had to endure, no matter the pain no matter the loneliness 'that my father would always be with me and that everything would be all right.

I learned that day that being single is a state of mind because to be single means to be the only one, or alone. The Bible teaches us that God is omnipresent, which means he is everywhere at the same time. This means that we are never alone or the only one. Being single loses most of its power when you know that even "it" cannot cause us to ever be alone.

I would have never in a million years thought that the darkest, loneliest moment of my life would also be the most comforting.

The word of God teaches us to be satisfied where we are.

1 Corinthians 7:27 (NIV)

²⁷ Are you married? Do not seek a divorce. Are you unmarried? Do not look for a wife.

God knows where we are and what position we are in. When we give our life to Christ, we turn it over to him. God wants us to focus on him, not on where we are or where we want to be.

Accepting Christ as your Savior is like getting on a bus. There is no one on the bus but you; you sit at the back of the bus, and Jesus is the driver. "Why at the back of the bus," you ask. Easy. The closer you sit to the driver, the more you have a tendency to question and react to the route. At the back of the bus, you are forced to have faith and trust the driver. Faith is not always easy, but that is the question: do you really trust him?

Here is what we have to do. First, honestly ask yourselves if you have truly given God total control of your life; if so, wherever you are has to be where God has brought you. If you are in an uncomfortable or painful place, there is a reason for it. Everything God does or allows has a purpose, so if you are single, and he is driving, then at this moment, single is where you should be. God will sometimes give us the desires of our heart, but he does not want us to focus on them. You will be amazed what God will give you when you stop trying so hard to get it. If you find this hard to do, move back, you are sitting too close.

Just because God is driving does not mean that the roads will not sometimes be bumpy, but relax, you're in good hands. If you have not given him total control, don't relax; in fact, *panic now*! And get on that bus.

It has been society that has portrayed that being single has something negative because nowhere does the Bible ever portray being single as something less than normal or less desirable. The Bible does not speak of singles as incomplete people who need marital partners to complete them.

On the contrary, the Scriptures tend to praise singles. One way the Bible uplifts being single for God's people is the sheer inclusion of so many prominent Bible characters that were single for life or widowed without remarriage. Among these godly singles were Elijah, Daniel, Jeremiah, John the Baptist, Jesus, Paul, Barnabas as well as widows like Naomi in the Book of Ruth, and Anna, the saintly woman who was 84 years of age when the Baby Jesus was dedicated in the Temple. Here is God's advice (*advice, not law*) given to us through his apostle Paul in 1 Corinthians 7:8:

1 Corinthians 7:8 (NIV)

8 Now to the unmarried and the widows I say: It is good for them to stay unmarried, as I am

It is important not to misinterpret this scripture. God is not saying not to get married; he is simply saying you may be in a better place as it pertains to your relationship with him if you don't. God also said in the ninth verse of that same chapter that if you cannot handle being single, you should get married.

1 Corinthians 7:9 (NIV)

9 But if they cannot control themselves, they should marry, for it is better to marry than to burn with passion.

If you do decide to get married, the concept of the bus should still apply. This means that like your church, your spouse should be appointed and not selected. If you are sitting too close, you will have all these wants and desires and say, "I want him or her to look like this, walk like that, have this much money, or drive that." The problem is that it may be the spouse *you* want but not the one *God* has for you. God, sometimes, gives the most perfect gift, but we never receive it because we don't like the wrapping paper it comes in. If you are sitting at the back of the bus, all you want is whatever God has for you, you have no expectations because you trust God and realize that whomever and whatever he sends you will be what is best for you.

If all this negative talk about being single is not you, and you are single, happy, and loving, having a relationship with Jesus with limited distractions, then good for you because in being single, you may be in the most accessible place you will ever be.

The Trials of Life

G od does not do anything *to* you but *for* you. I heard this many years ago, and it has helped me deal with so many of the trials and hard times that came in my life. It was easy to accept it as truth because God said it in the book of Romans.

Romans 8:28 (King James Version)

28 And we know that all things work together for good to them that love God, to them who are called according to his purpose.

Notice God said *all* things, which means even the things we consider bad are in some way working for good.

So why do so many trials come into our lives? If we accept Christ as our Savior, should he not protect us from trials? (*Well, at least that was my first thought*) But the truth is, trials are part of the "all things" that the Bible talks about in verse 28.

Romans 8:28 also lets us know that trials are not bad because it says *all* things work for good. If you are a Christian when God said "to them that love God and are called according to his purpose," that's you.

When we study the Bible, we learn at least three reasons as to why trials and hard times come into our lives.

The first reason is to discipline us. The second is to strengthen an area in our life where we might be weak. The third and most controversial one is service. Service is controversial because its circumstances can make it hard to deal with, it may also be the least frequent. Service means that the trial is not about you at all, the circumstances of the trial, or the testimony that comes after the trial, is to glorify God in a completely separate area. Let's look closer.

Discipline

You did what! OK, you are going to get a spanking, haven't we all heard this? And what about this one—"I am going to spank you because I love you"? Even though that last statement did not give us much comfort, it was true. It was true then, and it's true still today. God does sometimes discipline us. He does not like it anymore than we do when we discipline our own children, but he does it for the same reason . . . love.

God talks about judging, which is a form of his discipline.

1 Corinthians 11:31 (New International Version)

³¹But if we judged ourselves, we would not come under judgment.

God is simply saying, "Do as I have called and commanded you to do". Be obedient to my word, and you will not have to be disciplined. Some people reject the notion of God disciplining us because they think that because God is so loving and merciful, surely he would not do anything to hurt us. It is true that God will never do anything "to" hurt you, but he will allow things to happen in your lives to help you that "may" hurt you. Because many people do not understand this, they ignore whatever God does in their lives, blame the devil, and do nothing. Always remember the devil has no power in your life. He can only do what God allows him to . . . and if he does allow it, *it is for a reason.* God has all power in our lives. He is our father, and sometimes, fathers discipline their children. Verse 32 of 1 Corinthians, Chapter 11, tells us why God sometimes has to discipline us.

32When we are judged by the Lord, we are being disciplined so that we will not be condemned with the world.

This tells us that trails can be a form of judgment, which is at times used as a disciplinary action. So let's just say trials can sometimes be a spiritual spanking.

Trials Come to Make Us Strong

Probably the most common reason for trials is to strengthen weak areas of our life. Jesus tells us this in 1 Peter.

1 Peter 1:6-7 (New International Version)

6In this you greatly rejoice, though now for a little while you may have had to suffer grief in all kinds of trials. 7These have come so that your faith—of greater worth than gold, which perishes even though refined by fire—may be proved genuine and may result in praise, glory and honor when Jesus Christ is revealed.

As we mentioned earlier, God knows that spiritual things can sometimes be difficult in this worldly environment, and some of us may not accept things as fast as others. We know that God is merciful, holy, loving, and kind, but the two characteristics that we should be extremely thankful that he has is forgiveness and patience.

God's patience and forgiveness come from his love for us. How fortunate are we to have a father that loves us in spite of the fact that we are so undeserving, sometimes ungrateful, and always unworthy!

It is that love that causes God to be so patient and to forgive us over and over again. If anything we could do to another human had the effect that sin has on God, we would all be alone.

One of the reasons God is so patient is that he is not moved by time. That may also explain how certain trials seem to last a lifetime to us, but because God dwells in eternity, it's only a blink to him. God does not get any joy from the pain and discomfort that can come from the trials that we experience. He loves us so much that there is no amount of time he is not willing to spend, punishment he is not willing to dish out, or obstacle he is not willing to move to make sure we get whatever he has for us. We have to have faith in his word; though trials may sometimes be painful, they are always beneficial in the end.

One of the mistakes many of us make during a trial is to pray that God will end it as soon as possible—often before its purpose has been fulfilled. The perception is, "It was God that allowed this trial to come into my life, and it will only end when 'he' wants it to." We are just weak and powerless victims that have no other option but to pray, endure, and wait. Pray and wait is a common perception. The reality is that sometimes, we can do more. God's word has given us the wisdom and knowledge we need first of all to not get ourselves into many of these situations and has also empowered us to be able to change some of them. Consider this . . . You spank your child for something he continues to do, or you spank him for something he continues not to do . . . in both these situations, it is the child who has power over the spankings. This tells us that more often than not, we cause the situations we are in. Let's use faith as an example. Let's say you are struggling in this area. After all, Hebrews 11:1 says—

(New King James Version)

¹ Now faith is the substance of things hoped for, the evidence of things not seen.

In this verse, it's the things not seen that most of us struggle with. Because God does not usually reveal himself to us the way he sometimes did in the Bible (*he doesn't talk to us like he did to Paul on the road, or show us a burning bush like he did to Moses on the mountain*), all we have is faith. God knows that without complete faith in him, to walk with him will be impossible. So if he has to remove everything and everyone in our lives that we depend on to show us how important total dependence in him is, he will, and that may hurt us, but it's because he loves us so much that no sacrifice is too high for him to make for us. Remember Jesus?

The sooner we understand what God expects from us, and decide to be obedient to his word, the more power we will have over what God does, and does not have to take us through.

Remember, when it comes to God strengthening a certain area of our lives, or him having to discipline us, we are never waiting on him to end the trial, but he's always waiting on us.

From Test To Testimony

When we accept Christ as our Savior, we become his servant, and we are to be used in any way our master (God) chooses. Sometimes, God allows us to go through certain things to benefit others, but ultimately, he is always glorified.

Think about the book of Job. Job is the story of a righteous man who loved God and was very obedient to him. But God allowed him to go through some very hard trials for what at first seemed like a very unfair reason. When I first read the book of Job, the story was very confusing to me. I could not understand why God would allow a good and righteous man like Job to go through so much; he seemed so undeserving. At first, it seemed as if Jesus was doing it to prove a point to Satan. I thought how God could be so unfair. Was not Job's life worth more than Satan's? After all, the Bible tells us that Job was a righteous man who loved God and that the devil was evil and betrayed him. It seemed to me that Job was being punished for being obedient to God. At that point in my life, I was a new Christian, and this tested my faith. For over a year, I went back and forth on this issue, and the devil tried to turn me away from God. He kept asking, "Do you think you are more righteous than Job? If God will turn his back on Job, will he not do the same to you?" So I prayed for God to give me understanding on this issue. He revealed to me that he did not choose Job because he was not righteous enough. He chose him because he was. He then revealed to me that nothing Job went through was for him nor was it about the devil. Job was tested so that his life could be a testimony for all of us. It is important we keep this in mind. Job was not singled out, but he was selected for a specific job that would bring glory to God.

God has given us all *free will*, but he knows the nature of our hearts. So when he selects one of us for a job, he selects someone whom he can trust and someone who can handle the situation. Sometimes, he may even use someone that is not even a Christian. The apostle Paul is an example of this. Paul was born in the Greek city of Tarsus where he studied Judaism, which opposed some Christian beliefs. Paul was extremely committed and devoted to what he believed and was very zealous in defending it. Although Paul was not yet a Christian, God knew that because of his commitment to what he believed in, he could use Paul to glorify his kingdom. Some of you may be thinking that it sounds like Paul did not have free will, that it sounds like God selected him and that he did not have a choice. (*I did*), but God is Alpha and Omega, the beginning and the end, so he has the gift of divine prophecy, which means he knows everything. God did not make Paul accept him by selecting him; he selected him because he knew that he would.

So you see, Paul, like Job, was the man for the job. Just like God knew that he could use Paul, he also knew that Job's life would serve as a motivation and an inspiration for the rest of us. God wanted to show us how important it is to keep our focus on him and our faith in him and to remind us that he will never put more on us than we can bear. Remember, it's not always about you. God had to take Job down to his knees so that you and I could stand.

What an awesome privilege to be used by God in such a mighty way!

Ask yourself this question . . . what if you had to die so that everyone else could live? Would you? Jesus did. We were all created to be his servant, and because God does not need any of us, we should be honored.

Know that our God is a just God. He loves us more than any human is capable, and he will not take you through something for nothing.

Spiritual Perspective on Worldly Issues

What does the word say? Sounds easy enough, right? But it is amazing that when faced with giving an opinion on a worldly issue, how some Christians respond with something that is a total contradiction to what the word of God says. So why is this? I believe it is because we as (*Christians*) sometimes feel as though we have to walk a very thin line between the perceptions of the world and realities of Christianity.

It is as if we don't want to offend the world, even at the expense of not defending God.

As in so many others areas in our lives, we want to choose when we will stand up for God. If it's convenient, or benefits us, we will speak up. If our response is controversial or unpopular, we'll plead the fifth.

Remember Peter (*the disciple who denied Jesus*)? When it was safe, he acknowledged Jesus as his Savior, and when he felt danger, he denied he even knew him. Another reason we are sometimes less likely to respond spiritually on worldly issues is we feel as though our response could damage our position or image. This usually happens at work or in politics.

Let's say you are confronted with a question about your position on an immoral issue which the Bible calls a sin. You are against it because God is against it. But because it is an unpopular stance, you are unwilling to express your true feelings. Though this example is just hypothetical, it does reflect how we sometimes respond, and here is what Jesus says about this.

Matthew 10:33 (King James Version)

³³But whosoever shall deny me before men, him will I also deny before my Father which is in heaven.

Another reason we sometimes have different perspectives than God is that we often think about how the issue makes us feel personally. For example, if someone who is not in our family or close to us wants to do something that goes against God's will because it will not directly affect us, we are OK with it. But if we abide in God and he in us, how can we be for something he is against? You may think to yourself, *Just because I am not against something does not mean I am for it.*

The truth is, when it pertains to things of God, that is exactly what it means.

Whenever we are faced with a situation where we have to respond to something controversial, take an unpopular stance, or make a decision that may make us feel isolated, never let personal feelings, emotion, or the popular choice guide our responses or actions; just do what the word says.

It is better to stand with God alone, than to stand with everyone else without him.

The movie God is not dead *(great movie)* is a great example of this point. The main character plays a college student who stands up to his atheist professor to defend the existence of God even at the risk of losing everything and everyone around him.

The one thing we can never compromise on is the word of God; it doesn't matter who it offends. I realize that may be a strong position, but sometimes, in our efforts not to offend man, we offend God. Christians must defend God's word because the rest of the world will try to rationalize things that are wrong by focusing the attention on something else. They will focus on things like the right to have freedom of choice. This is a strategy society has used for years, but unfortunately, it has proven to be effective. What happens is that when someone or some group lobbies to have the society accept something that is spiritually and morally wrong, the attention is diverted to freedom of choice. It is effective because all of us can appreciate freedom. As we said earlier, freedom of choice is one of the greatest tools God gave man. Even though man does have the right to make his own choices, Christians also have the right and responsibility to stand against the things society accepts that go against the word of God.

The word of God has to be respected, obeyed, and sometimes defended. As Christians, there will be times when we will have to be strong and have the courage to stand up for what we believe in, no matter what the opposition. Because if not us, who.

Marriage: Learning to Walk Alone While Standing Together

Genesis 2:18 (NIV)

¹⁸ *The LORD God said, "It is not good for the man to be alone. I will make a helper suitable for him."*

Proverbs 18:22

²² *He who finds a wife finds what is good and receives favor from the LORD.*

1 Corinthians 7:1

¹*Now for the matters you wrote about: It is good for a man not to marry*

1 Corinthians 7:32

³²I would like you to be free from concern. An unmarried man is concerned about the Lord's affairs—how he can please the Lord

Here we have four different scriptures about marriage and two different perspectives, and if not studied properly, some could interpret them to be contradictory.

The reality is that these four scriptures summarize two very different aspects of marriage. We will study the first two and call them standing together, then we will look at the second two and call them walking alone.

Standing Together

God said in Genesis 2:24 that for his wife, a man will leave his father and mother, and they will become one flesh (*paraphrased, not quoted*). So how can a man and a woman become one flesh? There are three things that will be essential in accomplishing this, and we've mentioned them before, but one thing you will notice about your Christian walk is that there are some fundamental things that will consistently be at the center of your walk as a Christian. Again, they are things like love, faith, obedience, and trust. To become one flesh, we will need all of them, but let's focus on just three—love, trust, and obedience.

Love

Love of God and self.

Becoming one flesh, like most things, is first and foremost a choice. It is a choice because it cannot happen physically, only mentally.

Because we were created in Gods image to truly love yourself is to love God and vice versa. The love and respect we have for God and ourselves will ultimately outweigh anything else, which means the order of love has to be God, self, and then anyone else. Therefore, before we can become one with our spouse, we must first become one with God. This means that truly becoming one will depend far more on our relationship with God than that of our spouse.

Trust

Trust in God and the God that is within your spouse.

Whenever we put our trust and faith in people, we have to deal with flesh and emotions which can be unreliable. When we put our faith in Jesus, we rely on his love and grace because he is always faithful. So never put all your trust and faith in your spouse, but rather in the spirit of God that lives within them.

Obedience

Obedience to the word of God.

God is love, so whatever he tells us to do will always be what is best for us; so when in doubt, ask yourself what God would want you to do.

God believes in divine order, which is God first and man second.

The word of God teaches us that the man should submit to God and the wife to her husband.

The Bible also teaches us how we should relate to our spouses.

Husbands

Ephesians 5:25-28 (New International Version)

25Husbands, love your wives, just as Christ loved the church and gave himself up for her 26to make her holy, cleansing her by the washing with water through the word, 27and to present her to himself as a radiant church, without stain or wrinkle or any other blemish, but holy and blameless. 28In this same way, husbands ought to love their wives as their own bodies. He who loves his wife loves himself.

Wives

Ephesians 5:22-24 (New International Version)

22Wives, submit to your husbands as to the Lord. 23For the husband is the head of the wife as Christ is the head of the church, his body, of which he is the Savior. 24Now as the church submits to Christ, so also wives should submit to their husbands in everything.

One of the things I have learned about marriage is how amazingly easy it can be when we understand our roles. We should view our spouses the way God does, which is as a gift. I will share a personal testimony that I think will be a good example of this point. Years ago, my wife and I were not in a good place in our marriage. We were arguing often and considering a divorce. We were spending most of our time pointing fingers at each other, and we both felt as though we were not the problem. We thought the only answer was for the other to change. Because we did not see each other through the eyes of God, we did not realize that a gift from God should never be a problem (*God does not like it when we see his blessings as curses*) and that the problem was really within ourselves and the solution was in Christ. God revealed to us that the only person whose actions we have control over is ourselves and that our spouses were *his* job.

Consider this. How would you feel if someone comes to your house and says they want to discipline your kids because you are not doing a good enough job? "Yea right." Well, that is how God feels when we try to discipline his children, and your spouse is *his* child.

I'm sure most of you have heard this before, but I will put a little twist on it to make my point.

God grant *me* the serenity to accept the things I cannot change. (my spouse), courage to change the things I can (me), and wisdom to know the difference.

Once we learned and accepted this and got out of God's way by focusing on ourselves and surrendering our spouses to God, he changed everything and truly blessed our marriage.

The level of our commitment to someone is based on how important that person is to us, which is usually determined by how much we love them. Unfortunately, many of us feel that spouses are replaceable, that love will come, go, and come again, and that Jesus will always forgive. This mentality may explain the high divorce rate, even among Christians. Because of this, it is important that our true commitment is to something higher and greater than our marriage and our spouses, and that should be our covenant and God.

Marriage will not always be easy; it will require compromise, sacrifice, being submissive, obeying the ways of God, and most importantly, you will have to be spiritually, mentality, and emotionally *committed to your covenant with God first.*

This is prioritizing and positioning, and these are two very important aspects of a successful marriage.

Prioritizing is simply to just make sure that Jesus and *his* will is first in your life.

Positioning is knowing your role and what is expected of you, but know that properly prioritizing your life will help you get into position.

Our most effective position in our marriage will be to love our spouse through God. To do this, we have to use what I call triangle love. (*This concept came to me about four years ago, but it has been effective.*) Picture a triangle; it has three points: one on top and two on the sides. Notice that unlike other shapes, all points are connected to each other. If any point in the triangle is missing, it is no longer a triangle. This concept should be how we love in our marriage. You and your spouse represent the side points, and the top and always included has to be Jesus.

If we can accomplish these things, we can have the marriage "God" intended.

Walking Alone

When God said in 1 Corinthians 1:1 that it is good for a man not to marry, it was because he knew that it would be hard to walk alone while standing together.

Here is the reality (*brace yourself as this may be shocking*). We were not created to be spouses, parents, Coe's, millionaires, or any of the many titles we can attain in this world, but we were created to be worshipers and servants.

Here is the problem: if we are not very careful, life's titles and possessions can be a distraction.

Jesus warned us of this in 1 Corinthians 7:29-31.

(NIV)

> *29What I mean, brothers, is that the time is short. From now on those who have wives should live as if they had none; 30those who mourn, as if they did not; those who are happy, as if they were not; those who buy something, as if it were not theirs to keep; 31those who use the things of the world, as if not engrossed in them. For this world in its present form is passing away.*

The Bible then goes on to explain these verses.

1 Corinthians 7:32-35 (New International Version)

> *32I would like you to be free from concern. An unmarried man is concerned about the Lord's affairs—how he can please the Lord. 33But a married man is concerned about the affairs of this world—how he can please his wife—34and his interests are divided. An unmarried woman or virgin is concerned about the Lord's affairs: Her aim is to be devoted to the Lord in both body and spirit. But a married woman is concerned about the affairs of this world—how she can please her*

> *husband.* [35]*I am saying this for your own good, not to restrict you, but that you may live in a right way in undivided devotion to the Lord.*

The goal is to be able to be devoted to God to the point where he is undoubtedly first in our lives. *The question* is, can we be devoted to the Lord while wearing many worldly titles? *The challenge* is to do them both.

Let's go back to becoming one flesh for a moment. Think about Siamese twins, two different individuals joined together becoming one flesh. When a man and his wife become one flesh, their life should mimic that of the Siamese twins.

Because they are one flesh, the Siamese twins have to permanently (*until death parts them*) coexist in the same environment, which causes them to have to be in agreement with each other, to be sensitive to the feelings and needs of the other, and in most cases, without considering the option of physical separation (*divorce*). Because they are joined,(*marriage*) they can only separate in their minds.

Separating in our minds is a must for all married couples because it is the only place where we can walk alone.

Walking alone simply means to have a separate and individual relationship with God that is outside of the one you share with your spouse.

It is very important that we understand our judgment position, which is on our knees, and *alone*. God will not judge Mr. and Ms John Doe as a couple; he will judge them as individuals. When he judges Mr. Doe, it is very possible that Ms Doe's name will not even come up because he will be judged on the merit of his *individual* relationship with the father.

This is probably even more important to wives because some may misinterpret God's word and believe that because God said that a woman is to submit to her husband in every way and that the husband is to cover the wife, the wife may, in some way, be vindicated on judgment day because of what her husband did or did not do. This is false, for the woman will be judged in the same way the man will, on her *own* merit.

Neither of us will be able to say on that day, "Lord, I did not serve you because of her," or, "Lord, I was not obedient to you because of him," or the conversation will be between *you* and *your* father, about *you* and *your* father.

This is important because sometimes we have a tendency to get so caught up with sharing everything with our spouses that we lose sight of the fact that though we may share praising, worshiping, witnessing and serving with our spouse, our *relationship* with God must be an *individual* one. It is because of this that the greatest day of divorce known to man may be the Rapture. Husbands and wives will separate and go in two different directions because one understood and the other did not, that Jesus has to have one place and one position in our lives, *first.*

God has laid out a blueprint for every aspect of our lives in the Bible, a ten-step program if you will, but know that if you don't follow *every* step, you will not get the desired result for *any.*

Religion and Relationship

This may very well be the most important chapter in this book, or maybe it's just the one I am most passionate about.

Have you ever loved someone with all your heart and wanted nothing more than to know that the feeling was mutual? After all, is not the greatest thing about loving someone knowing that they love you too? Picture this. You love someone with everything inside you, and because of his or her words or actions, you are positive they love you too. Then one day you realize you were wrong, not about their love, but about yours.

You may think, *Oh sure, I have called lust love before or had a strong attraction for someone and thought it was love.* This happens all the time, and it proves we know the difference between really loving someone and some kind of infatuation, but what about Jesus? How do we know that we truly love him?

To love Jesus is to know him, and to know him is to have a relationship with him. The difference between knowing him and

69

knowing of him can very easily be an example of the difference between religion and a relationship.

Unfortunately, many people believe there is little or no difference between the two. Sure, if you ask them, they will tell you they are different. If asked what the evidence of their salvation is, they may say, "I believe in God, I go to church every Sunday, I serve in church, I am a deacon or an elder, and I always tell people about God." All these things are good, but they all fall under the category of religious works and are not the evidence of a relationship.

Having religion in your life and having a relationship with God is very different. Study will show that religion is man-made. When I looked up the definition of the word religion, I found no consensus on its meaning. The "web" defines religion as a strong belief in a supernatural power or powers that control human destiny.

Holman's Bible Dictionary gives several meanings. One is—a fear of God, and it tells us that the Greek root of the word suggests freely chosen worship. Notice all these definitions define the idea of religion but not the method. Method is the practice or procedure of doing something, which, as it pertains to religion, is usually different because man defines it.

Man's method of religion is usually based on man trying to get close to God and into heaven through rules, regulations, personal beliefs, and works. When summarized, it means man's own efforts.

It is important to understand that having and practicing religion accomplishes neither. We get to heaven because of God's grace and close to him with a *personal* relationship. Can you have one without the other? Can you make it to heaven without a personal relationship? Can you have a personal relationship and not go to heaven? Some think all you have to do is believe that Jesus is who he said he was, and others acknowledge a need for a relationship but confuse it with religion. If making the decision to follow Christ is the most important decision you will ever make, then knowing the difference between practicing religion and having a relationship with father has to be second. If you spend your whole life trying to be the most religious person on earth without a relationship, you will be no closer to spending eternity with Christ than a common atheist.

Let's look at the consequences of confusing having religion with having a relationship.

Matthew 7:21-33 (KJV)

Not everyone who says to me, "Lord, Lord," will enter the kingdom of heaven, but only he who does the will of my Father who is in heaven. [22] *Many will say to me on that day, "Lord, Lord, did we not prophesy in your name, and in your name drive out demons and perform many miracles?"* [23] *Then I will tell them plainly, "I never knew you. Away from me, you evildoers!"*

In the above scripture, God uses the phrase, I never *knew* you. In Hebrew, the word "know" is defined as intimacy, and intimacy is a relationship. Of all the scriptures in the Bible, the saddest and most fearful are the very words that come from Jesus himself in these three scriptures. In them, Jesus is telling us that on judgment day, there will be some people who will fully expect to ascend to heaven with him in the clouds of glory, but he will have to tell them, *"Depart from me. I never knew you." Again, make no mistake about it. There will be people on the Day of Judgment who would be expecting to go to heaven; yet, instead of inheriting the kingdom, they will hear those saddening words, "Depart from me. I never*

71

knew you." *There will be deacons, Sabbath schoolteachers, elders, pastors, TV evangelists, and miracle workers along with countless others (i.e. all church people) that will be turned away because they lacked one very necessary qualification—they did not truly know the Lord.* The people Jesus will say he "never knew" will be those who never felt the need to truly "know him." Yet these are people who "think" they are going to heaven. Let's look deeper at the concept of knowing someone and knowing *of* someone. Here's an example: You may know that the name of the president of the United States is Barack Obama, that he graduated from Harvard University, that he is married to Michelle and that has two children named Sasha and Malia. Now if the two of you were in the presence of someone who did not know either of you, it would appear that you knew President Obama because of your knowledge of him. In the same way, we may know the story of Jesus, but it does not mean we know him. Here are some other examples of the differences between Religion and Relationship the.

Religion can be a series of man-made procedures that satisfies the individual into thinking that growth is taking place.

Relationship with Christ produces growth as you get closer to him and strive to emulate him.

Religion will often ask you to accept things without question because of tradition

Relationship with Christ causes you learn more about him and all the questions "that you need to know" will be answered.

Religion sometimes praises ministers, pastors, and elders as the only ones who are to spread the word of God.

Relationship teaches us that we are all part of his church and are all called to be his disciples.

Religion can teach us to follow.

A relationship teaches us to lead.

Religion is evidence.

Relationship is proof.

Religion will not make you obedient.

Relationship will encourage and motivate you honor and obey the word of God

All of us would agree that relationships are not easy. We have to make time for them, we make sacrifices because of them, and we have to be passionate while in them. Many relationships fail because they cannot handle the distractions that sometimes hinder our efforts to nurture the relationship properly. Here are some things that can hinder our relationship with Christ. When we think of distractions, the things that we usually think of (or *maybe that we will admit to*) are things like disobedience, greed, envy, sin, and pride just to name a few. But this list is easy, for even a unbeliever would agree with them. One of the reasons we may be so quick to identify these distractions is because we feel like they don't describe us; after all, these are not common character traits for Christians. Some Christians do struggle with these things, and they can be a distraction from a relationship with Christ, but commonly, the distractions that we face are things like our careers, personal life goals, ambition, and life itself. Most of us will admit to those things, and we are quick to say that none of them are more important than our relationship with Christ. If we realize they are, we will repent, reposition, and prioritize our lives and move on. OK, that would work, but what about our families, our spouse, or our children? What if they are the reason we are distracted? What if sometimes we hold them to a higher regard than Christ and not even realize it, this is another reason why God made it a point to caution us about family in 1corinthians 7:32-35

We discussed the impact families can have on our lives temporarily and eternally. Since this is the second time they've come up, I feel I should elaborate. If I may be clear, families are a beautiful and wonderful gift God has allowed us to have and enjoy; they bring so much love and peace into our lives that we would undoubtedly feel lost without them, but we have to be very careful of the position we give to anyone or anything in our lives because we serve a very jealous God, and anything or anyone that we hold in a higher regard than Christ will definitely hinder and distract us from a relationship with him.

One mistake we often make is we try to love our worldly relationships "with God," meaning we love them equally. None of us will admit to this, but our actions will show it is what we do. This causes our interest to be divided. Here is what happens when we do this. When you love someone "with God," you put them "next to God" which makes them "equal to God," so now God is not "the God" of your life but "a God" in your life. We know that the first commandment tells us not to have any other gods before him, and the Bible also says in Isaiah 45:11, I alone am God and beside me there is no other.

The only way we can develop and nurture a relationship with Christ is when we put him first.

Proof and Evidence

There is a distinct difference between evidence of salvation and proof of salvation.

Evidence—that which is helpful in forming a conclusion or judgment.

Proof—evidence sufficient enough to establish a thing as true.

If a man goes to church every Sunday, reads the Bible every day, and serves in church on Wednesdays, those around him may see these things as proof of his salvation. He also may think his place in eternity is secure because of what he does. The reality is, though all those things are good, and ultimately pleasing to God, they are not proof of salvation; they are only evidence, and all of them are considered works. The Bible teaches us we are not saved by works but by grace. Some interpret that to mean that they get some sort of free pass—that they don't have to do anything but accept and believe that Christ is who he said he was and did what the Bible says he did. But think about it. If that was all we needed to do to be saved, would not Satan and all his demons be in heaven? Does Satan not believe that Jesus is who he said he is and know that he did everything the Bible says? We have to know that simply believing is not enough.

God said in Matthew 7:22—

²²Many will say to me on that day, "Lord, Lord, did we not prophesy in your name and in your name drive out demons and perform many miracles?

In this passage of scripture, who is the Lord talking to? Sinners and unbelievers don't prophesy in his name, and they don't drive out demons or perform miracles. In this scripture, God is talking to people who profess Christ as their Savior. People who themselves believe, and everyone around them who believe, are dying and on their way to heaven. It is not enough to know *of* God and be able to tell his story; we have to *know* him. *Knowing him comes from having a relationship with him. Our salvation depends on it.*

I realize that most of us believe that all we have to do to be saved is to acknowledge that Jesus is the Son of God and that he did die on the cross for our sins. The reality is that acknowledgment is more than just a statement. True acknowledgment is a relationship.

So how can I be sure I have a relationship with God? How can I be sure that when I kneel before the father, he will not say to me, "Depart from me. I never you"? What is proof of my salvation? Jesus said, "You will know them by their fruit."

John 15:5 (NIV)

⁵ *"I am the vine; you are the branches. If a man remains in me and I in him, he will bear much fruit; apart from me you can do nothing."*

Message from Our Father

Revelation 22:12-17 (NIV)

¹² "Behold, I am coming soon! My reward is with me, and I will give to everyone according to what he has done. ¹³ I am the Alpha and the Omega, the First and the Last, the Beginning and the End.

¹⁴ "Blessed are those who wash their robes, that they may have the right to the tree of life and may go through the gates into the city. ¹⁵ Outside are the dogs, those who practice magic arts, the sexually immoral, the murderers, the idolaters and everyone who loves and practices falsehood.

¹⁶ "I, Jesus, have sent my angel to give you this testimony for the churches. I am the Root and the Offspring of David, and the bright Morning Star."

¹⁷ *The Spirit and the bride say, "Come!" And let him who hears say, "Come!" Whoever is thirsty, let him come; and whoever wishes, let him take the free gift of the water of life.*

*The grace of our Lord Jesus Christ be
with you all. Amen.*

—Revelation 22:21